CARS

BY CHRISTOPHER PICK

Galley Press

CONTENTS

Previous page: interior view of the 1947 HRG sports car.

Left: 1917 6-cylinder Winton tourer, a seven-seat model produced in a basically unchanged form between 1909 and 1924.

INTRODUCTION

Railways had been in existence for nearly a century before motoring became anything but a rather idiosyncratic pastime confined to a wealthy few. Trains made it possible to travel more quickly and cheaply than ever before but on a train you could only go where the railway could take you. A car gives its owner more or less unlimited freedom to go where he wants and more or less unlimited flexibility as to when he should go. Add to this the close control that a driver has over the car – both over its successful mechanical functioning, much of which he can ensure himself, and over its behaviour on the road – and the power that he can literally feel under his feet, and something of the allure of the car becomes clear. But before we look at the various consequences of the automobile a little more closely, we need to go back to the earliest days of motoring, when car production was measured in single vehicles rather than hundreds, let alone hundreds of thousands.

Cars grew out of two other means of transport: trains and bicycles. A few steam carriages had been manufactured in the 1820s and 1830s as the railways were getting under way, but the experiments came to nothing, overwhelmed by the expanding railway network. In the 1860s, bicycles had come into fashion, reminding people of the pleasures of road travel and, more important, teaching engineers about the construction of light, strong structures. At about the same time, the internal combustion engine was invented. It was patented in 1860 by a Frenchman, Étienne Lenoir, who in 1863 drove a car from Paris to Vincennes and back. The six-mile journey took three hours (the vehicle had only $1\frac{1}{2}$ horsepower). Twelve years later, in Vienna, a vehicle belonging to an inventor named Siegfried Marcus made a sixteen-mile trip, travelling at 4mph.

As is often the case, the first tentative steps in motoring were made by men who became discouraged, lost interest or lacked the resources to continue. It was left to others to exploit the pos-sibilities. These were pre-eminently Gottlieb Daimler and Karl Benz, both Germans. Benz's three-wheeled car was produced in 1884; by 1888 more conventional cars were being manufactured, though at first it was hard to find buyers for them. Daimler developed a high-speed internal combustion engine and in 1885 built a motorcycle and a motorized carriage. Thereafter the story becomes more complex, involving manufacturers and engineers in different countries – chiefly France, Germany, Great Britain and the United States – experimenting widely and gradually resolving the technical problems.

Overcoming a sceptical public and hostile authorities was one of the main problems facing the motoring pioneers. At least as far as the first of these obstacles was concerned, motor races brought home the thrill of the open road to an enormous number of people. They also proved valuable for testing prototype vehicles.

The first race, held in 1895, was run from Paris to Bordeaux and back on ordinary roads; the fastest car – though for technical reasons not the victor – was a Panhard, driven by Émile Levassor at an average speed of 15mph. In 1896 cars raced from Paris to Marseilles and back and, as the century turned, more races were held over longer distances. In 1903, however, the Paris to Madrid race was halted at Bordeaux after a series of accidents and several deaths (the average speed of the declared winner was 65.3mph, 50mph higher than that achieved just eight years earlier). Thereafter races were confined to tracks and circuits; and racing cars too deviated more and more from the production models driven by motorists on the open road.

Hostile authorities were the main problem in the United Kingdom, where at first the speed of motor vehicles had been severely restricted (until 1896

The Ford Model T was the first mass-produced car and, before Volkswagen, the most successful.

4

to 4mph and in many places to 2mph) and where until about the mid-1900s even minor infringements of the law were severely, and frequently unfairly, punished.

But, over-eager policemen aside, motoring was very much an enthusiast's hobby in the early days. Cars were open, so driver and passengers had to wrap up well. Dust from the road was a major hazard, often obscuring the road, as were irate pedestrians, shying horses and barking dogs. Far worse, though, must have been the mechanical problems: diaries of early motorists reveal day after day spent trying to get the motor to start, or to repair it in mid-countryside (often with the help of the local blacksmith), or to find fuel of the correct density (no chains of service stations in those days) and only occasionally experiencing the triumph of a long stretch covered in record time.

None the less, motoring became more popular and the number of cars – 8000 in the United States in 1900, nearly 8500 in the United Kingdom in 1904 – increased rapidly. In England, Morris and Austin had started manufacturing before the beginning of World War I and in the United States Ford and General Motors were well under

way. Automobiles became established, driving them was rather less hair-raising, and in 1914 the question was how society would adapt, not whether it would.

In the 1920s, in the United States at least, car ownership was no longer unusual. In the 1928 presidential election, the Republican candidate, Herbert Hoover, promised voters not merely 'a full dinner pail' but 'a full garage' as well. In 1929 there were 26½ million cars on the road, one for every five people; production that year reached a record level (over five million). That year also brought the Wall Street crash, which hit the automobile industry particularly hard. Production slumped disastrously (a little over a million cars were made in 1932) and only slowly revived. Production totals in 1929 were not in fact exceeded until 1949, though interestingly enough the total number of cars on the road declined by only 10 per cent during the slump – an indication of how firmly entrenched motoring had become. These increases were repeated, on a smaller scale, in the United Kingdom in the 1930s. Morris went over to mass production in 1934, manufacturers vied with one another to produce the £100 car (and, though they only succeeded for a short

while, prices were kept remarkably low). The volume of traffic went up by 47 per cent between 1930 and 1935 and car registrations from 1,042,300 in 1929 to 2,134,000 ten years later.

But this was nothing compared with what happened once the last restrictions were removed after World War II. Again, statistics tell the story most vividly: 10,000 Volkswagen (Hitler's people's car, more fondly remembered as the 'beetle') were built in 1946, the millionth in 1955, the second millionth at the end of 1957, the fifth in 1962 and the fifteenth in 1972. World output of motor vehicles trebled between 1950 and 1970 from ten million to an incredible thirty million vehicles a year; in the United States in 1969 there were just 1.9 people for each vehicle. In western Europe also, two-car families are no longer unusual, especially since the introduction of the Mini – the first of a whole range of low-cost, low-consumption cars (nearly $4\frac{1}{2}$ million have now been sold).

Outside the favoured areas of the western world, car ownership has been slower to increase but now eastern Europe, Latin America and the more prosperous nations of the developing world are facing the problems that mass car ownership brings. And the extent of these problems should not be underestimated.

The growth of car ownership forced governments, some sooner, some later, to embark on programmes of motorway construction. While these fast routes have brought undoubted social benefits, their cost, and not merely in terms of cash expended, has been enormous. Road accidents take a frightening toll: 19,229 lives lost in the United Kingdom in 1976 and an estimated total financial loss of £1,290,000.

Perhaps equally serious is the crucial part that vehicle-manufacturing plays in the economies of the developed world. So many other industries and people live off the motor industry that governments simply cannot afford to let an ailing car concern go to the wall.

Man has indeed been freed from the limitations of his geography, but not without new and persistent problems to cope with. Yet there can be little doubt but that the invention and development of the motor car has had an impact which is little short of that of the invention of the wheel itself.

Opposite and below: an inter-war Mercedes and a modern Cadillac.

THE HORSELESS CARRIAGE

The term horseless carriage indicates how early motorists
viewed their cars – as mechanical extensions of their horse-
pulled vehicles. And it is clear from the vehicles'
appearances that their designers shared this view. It was
not immediately certain that cars would be petrol driven.
The 1914 Detroit Electric, below, was one of the most
successful of a range of electric cars available during the
1910s. It was still being made in the 1930s, though
production reached its peak between 1912 and 1920.
Opposite is the Ford Model A, the first car built by Henry
Ford as an independent manufacturer.

The 1903 Mercedes 60 (*above*) has been
described as the starting-point of all modern
automobile design. It won the 1903 Gordon
Bennett races in Ireland reaching an average
speed of 49.2mph and a maximum speed of
66mph. It also performed well in other
competitions. The stage was now set for the
rapid success of the Mercedes company, both in
racing and in the production of luxury, high-
performance cars, under the direction of Paul
Daimler and Emil Jellinek after whose
daughter, Mercedes, the company was named.

The 1912 Garros' Bugatti (*opposite, above*) was a
four-cylinder, five-litre racing car nicknamed
after Roland Garros, the French aviator who
bought the first of the three or four chassis
produced. Ettore Bugatti, who ranks as one of
the most influential designers and manufacturers,
exhibited his first car in 1901 and started
manufacturing on his own account in 1910.

Sizaire-Naudin produced the most successful
single-cylinder French *voiturettes* (small sports
cars) (*opposite below*). Designed by Maurice
Sizaire and built by his brother Georges and the
brothers Naudin, it appeared in 1905, won
its first major victory in 1906 and kept its
winning streak until 1909. By 1910, four-cylinder
voiturettes were being introduced and soon were
defeating the single-cylinder cars. The 1908
version shown here was the largest single-
cylinder Sizaire.

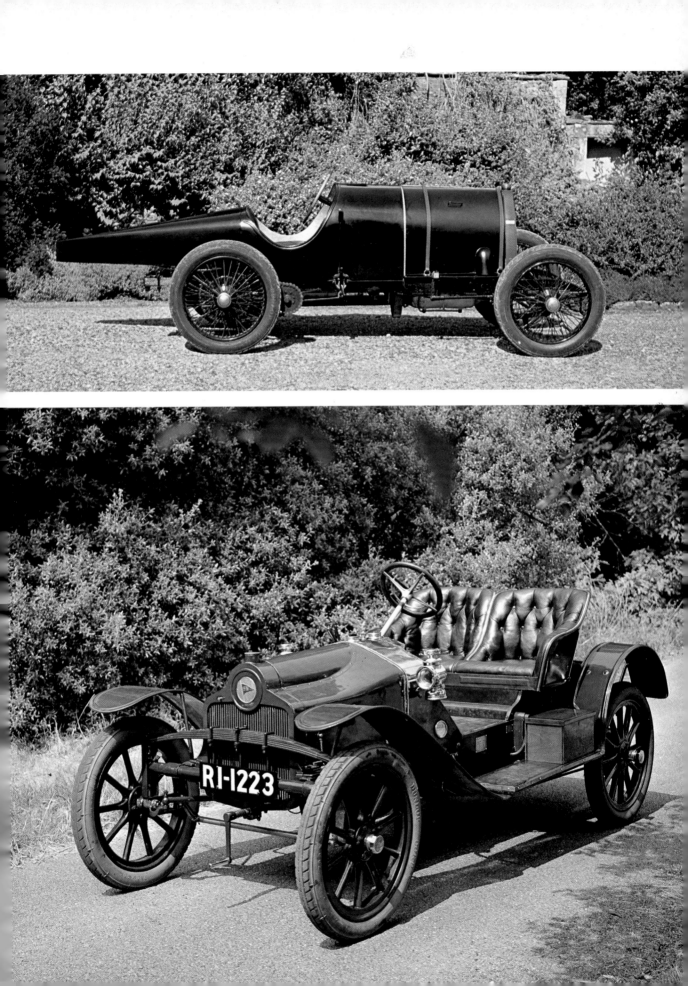

In the 1900s, Napiers were perhaps Britain's most luxurious cars, at least until the Rolls-Royce Silver Ghost (see page 18) had established itself. Manufacturing started in 1903 and almost immediately concentrated on six-cylinder models, which gave a smooth ride and were comfortable and easy to drive. Napier racing-cars, many of them simply stripped down versions of the touring models, were also successful. They gained a great deal of publicity for the company, especially after its sales director, S. F. Edge completed a 24-hour run at Brooklands, the motor course just south of London, at an average speed of 60mph in 1907. After Edge left the company in 1912, things were never quite the same, and production ceased during the 1920s. Shown here is a 1908 11.5 litre Napier.

Below is a 1912 Unic tourer. Unic (the company was started in 1905 by Frenchman Georges Richard) had a policy of manufacturing just one car – hence its name. In fact, within a year Richard had modified his ideas, and in 1914 he had three four-cylinder cars in production. The most famous was the 12/14, which was never available as a private car, but for many years served Londoners as taxis. It had a very small turning circle and was mechanically very sound, but without doors and a heater journeys must have been unpleasant for both the cabby and his fare. The tourers, built on similar lines, were never very successful. Unic is now part of the Fiat company.

A 1915 Dodge Four is shown below. This car was first produced in November 1914 and was the first car manufactured by the Dodge Brothers, Horace and John. Until then, their involvement in the motor industry had been as the very successful proprietors of the Detroit machine-shop in which Henry Ford's first engines were built. The Dodge Four was a market-leader right from the start: over 70,000 were delivered in 1916, when it was the fourth most popular car in the USA. It was also used as a First World War staff car and ambulance. Production continued until the mid-1920s. In 1928 Dodge was bought up by Chrysler, but the name is still used.

One of the more popular British cars immediately before the First World War was the twin-cylinder, eight-horsepower Perry, shown above. Production is thought to have continued into the first months of the war, and indeed in 1915 a larger version was announced, and a few were built. The car was re-announced, however, in 1919 by Bean (who had taken Perry over as part of an ambitious post-war expansion programme).

The 1913 tourer (*opposite*) was produced by one of Britain's oldest manufacturers, Lagonda. The car, a six-cylinder version of the four-cylinder Torpedo, was first produced in 1907. It won a gold medal in the 1910 Russian Reliability Trial held between Moscow and St Petersburg (now Leningrad). Tsar Nicholas became one of the car's greatest admirers and, before 1914, a considerable number were exported to Russia. Indeed, a substantial percentage of the company's sales went to that country until the 11.1 horsepower light car was introduced in 1913. Thereafter the company had a distinguished if chequered career. A take-over by Rolls-Royce in 1935 was successfully resisted, and, with W. O. Bentley as chief designer, the company remained independent until 1948.

Rolls-Royce

On the left and below are two Rolls-Royce Silver Ghosts dating from 1911 and 1914, respectively. Silver Ghosts, perhaps the most distinguished models from certainly the most distinguished motor manufacturer in the world, were produced between 1907 and 1926. In all, 7870 were built – 1700 in the United States, where, however, production ceased in 1931, after ten years, because American customers preferred their Silver Ghosts to be built in Britain.

The cars were reliable and silent – an early road report described the engine as 'a silent sewing machine' and travellers as being 'wafted through the landscape'. Silver Ghosts were named after chassis number 60551, the thirteenth six-cylinder 40–50hp Rolls-Royce to be built at the company's Manchester works. This vehicle was displayed at the 1906 Motor Show under the pet name The Silver Ghost, because the metal parts were silver plated, the body was finished in silver paint and the car ran extremely quietly. In the following year it performed outstandingly in various trials and more than doubled the record for distance covered without any involuntary stops to 14,371 miles. This particular car is still in existence, having covered well over half a million miles.

During the First World War, Silver Ghosts served as ambulances, staff cars and even as armoured cars.

CARRIAGE TO CAR

The inter-war years were perhaps the golden age of
motoring. Both manufacturers and motorists could put the
difficulties and discomforts of the pre-war years behind
them. The manufacturers could concentrate on producing
luxury vehicles for the upper end of the market, or
manufacturing cheap models for the already growing
number of family motorists. The motorists began to enjoy
the pleasures of travelling on a network of traffic-free roads.
This saloon is typical of the comforts of the time.

Roaring twenties

The Standard Avon Special (*opposite, top left*) is a two-seater sports car based on the popular 1930s family saloon, the Standard Nine, and converted by the coach-builders New Avon Body Company. Later Avons were built on various standard chassis from 9 to 20hp and were mostly four-seater tourers or saloons.

The Napier 40/50hp (*below*) was built between 1919 and 1924 in an unsuccessful attempt to displace Rolls-Royce. But only 187 were built and, in suspension, noise, brakes and handling, the car was slightly inferior to the Silver Ghost and the Hispano-Suiza. The coachwork, by Napier's subsidiary, Cunard, lacked elegance, too. Its maximum speed, 70mph, was, however, faster than the Silver Ghost.

Opposite, below left is a 1924 Trojan 10hp saloon. Trojan cars were a British attempt to produce reliable, easily maintained, cheap cars for a popular market, and although they did not sell as well as the Ford Model T or, later, the Volkswagen, they achieved the same high

standards. The Trojan was produced in 1922 and remained in production until 1936.

Top right: 1925 Delage V-12 2-litre Grand Prix racing car built by Louis Delage, one of the earliest French manufacturers. Delage entered a *voiturette* in the 1906 Coupe de l'Auto race, and remained prominent in racing circles until he withdrew in 1928. This first V-12 Grand Prix car made its appearance in 1923. Racing with limited success in that season and in the following one, it did better in 1925, providing a real, though not overwhelming, challenge to the then-dominant Alfa Romeo P2s.

In the Spanish Grand Prix, Delage cars took first, second and third places (although admittedly Alfa Romeo did not compete). A Delage also won first place in the French Grand Prix, after Alfa Romeo's withdrawal following a fatal crash. In 1926 this model was replaced by straight-eight 1½-litre cars.

Below right: a 1928 Citroën B14. André Citroën started manufacturing in 1919 and had immediate success, establishing himself within ten years as one of France's major manufacturers and opening factories in Britain, Italy and Germany.

Three hundred and fifty chain-driven two-seater sports cars like this 1926 Frazer Nash were produced between the mid-1920s and 1939. Developed out of the GN cycle car, the Frazer Nash had a simple, efficient and unique chain-driven transmission system. Each gear had a separate, exposed chain and sprockets. Their most successful competition years were 1930 to 1935. Despite their victories, they must be considered a blind alley as far as their contribution to future developments is concerned.

The Citroën Kegresse is a half-track
experimental military vehicle which was
produced in 1929. In the 1920s Citroën carried
out a good deal of work on the half-track
system, which had been originated by M.
Kegresse, formerly manager of Tsar Nicholas
II's garage. The system was installed chiefly on
commercial and military vehicles, but some
private cars were adapted, one of which was
used to make the first successful trans-Saharan
expedition by car in 1922–3.

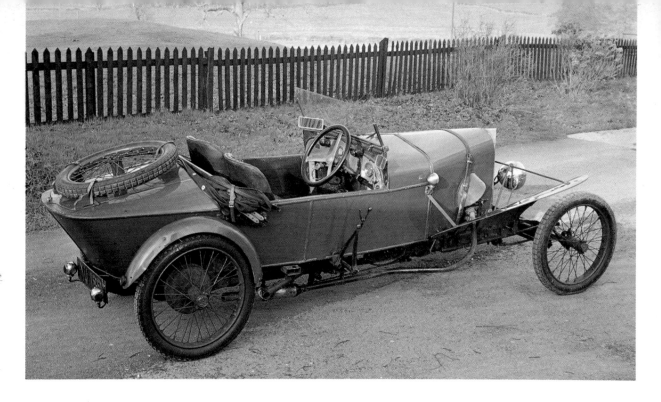

Cyclecars were developed from 1910 onwards in both France and Great Britain. They were halfway between a motorcycle and a car and fulfilled the demand for a really cheap vehicle. The 1913 Dewcar, for instance, cost as little as £60. The boom year was 1912, when there were over 70 different makes on display at the Motorcycle Show at London's Olympia exhibition halls.

Only three manufacturers survived the war, and they soon found themselves up against superior competition from the small cars being produced in considerable numbers in the 1920s. Price was no longer an advantage. The cyclecar shown above, for instance – a 1921 boat-tailed sporting GN – cost £315. Two years later the Austin Seven, which was more comfortable and gave better protection from the weather, came on the market at just over half that price.

GN, incidentally, was one of the main makes of cyclecar. The chassis was wooden, and the car had two-speed chain drive.

The 1920 Dodge (*opposite above*) is typical of the competitively priced cars which began to be produced in the 1920s.

Manufacture of the Seal three-wheeler started in 1912 and continued until 1924. The model shown on the right is a 1921 four-seater covered version. Although it was similar to a motorcycle and sidecar in looks it is in fact driven from the sidecar.

The original 1923 Alvis 12/50 racing car (*top*) was the first of a long line of successful 12/50s. It won several sprint races in the summer of that year, driven by Alvis's chief designer and engineer, Captain G. T. Smith-Clarke. Eight basic body types were manufactured, and the car did not go out of production until 1932. Below is the popular 'duck's back' version.

Opposite: the 1921 Horstmann 11hp Super Sports car was one of the range of Horstmann light cars. First manufactured in 1914, they became very popular in the 1920s. The racing models had front-wheel brakes installed in 1921 and supercharging was introduced two years later. The tourers were too expensive for their type and production stopped in 1929.

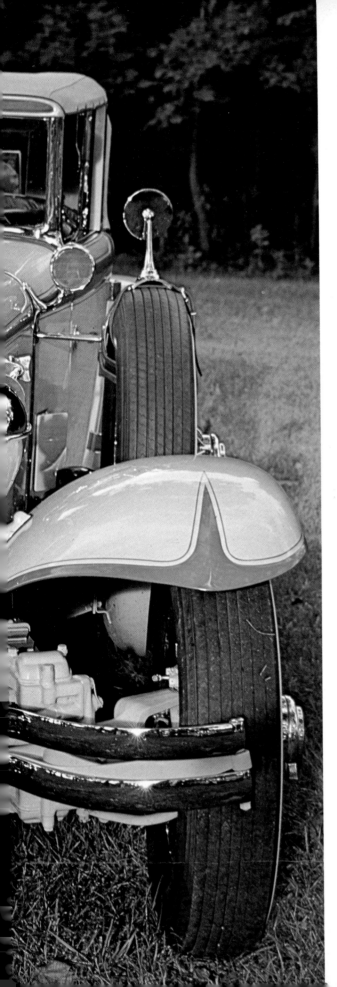

1930s

For those who could afford it, the 1930s brought the chance of super-comfort and super-elegance, qualities epitomized by Cadillac. The 'Standard of the World' was how the company proudly referred to itself. The V16 was launched in early 1930, hardly the most auspicious moment for such an automobile, and the V12 followed only a few months later. Externally the two models did not differ: the entire chassis and coachwork were common to both. Improvements were made throughout the 1930s: power brakes were introduced in 1931 and ride control the following year. No-draught ventilation arrived the year after that and all-steel bodies were made in 1935.

The one fact that more than any other speaks for Cadillac's success in these years is the sales record of the V12 and V16: 11,000 of the former and nearly 4000 of the latter in one decade, a startling achievement in the prevailing financial situation.

Below is a unique car, the 24-litre Napier Railton. It was built in 1933 to John Cobb's specification for track racing at Brooklands, and for attempts on the World 24-Hour Record. Almost at once it took the Brooklands lap record, reaching 120.59mph, and left it, never to be broken, at 143.44mph two years later. In 1935 the car took the World 24-Hour Record and the World Hour Record, the latter at 152.7mph. In 1933 it increased the 24-Hour Record to 160.6mph. Cobb stopped racing the car in 1937.

The 1933 supercharged MG K3 Magnette racing car (*opposite, top left*) is typical of the Magnette series produced between 1931 and 1935. The series consisted of saloons, two-seater sporting cars and the K3s, of which 34 were built. The Magnette performed well in the 1933 and 1934 seasons, Tazio Nuvolari driving one to take the Ulster TT in 1933.

The 1934 ERA racing car (*opposite, top right*) is the model that in 1935 provided the first challenge to the K3 Magnette. That year the ERA took first place in the Dieppe Grand Prix. In 1936 it was first at Monaco, and in 1937, its year of triumph, it scored fourteen victories. In

the following two seasons it had less success, though after the war it continued to be raced privately until 1951.

Bottom left: 1932 Bugatti Type 51a racing car. In the early 1930s, until the company withdrew from racing in 1934, Bugatti produced a number of racing cars. The Type 51, described as 'perhaps the most effective racing model' built by Bugatti, was introduced in 1931. It won six times that year and repeated its successes in 1932 and 1933.

The 1938 2-litre BMW 328 two-seater sports

car (*bottom right*) is strikingly styled and engineered. The 328 had considerable influence on post-war design and swept all before it in the many events it entered.

Overleaf: the Cord 812 came into production in 1937, the year the Cord company went out of business. It had front-wheel drive (Cords were the first such cars to be at all popular) and a 4.7-litre V-8 engine. A supercharged version was also available. The 812 and its sister, the 810, in manufacture since 1935, were both expensive at over $3500 and only 2320 of both versions were built.

CARS IN THE HEADLINES

Cars, motoring and motorists have never been far from the headlines for long. Indeed, newspapers did a good deal to promote cars in their earliest days. It was, for instance, the Chicago *Times Herald* that sponsored the first motoring contest in the USA in 1895, and the first races between international teams, for the Gordon Bennett Cup, were launched by James Gordon Bennett, owner of the *New York Herald*, in 1899. Just over 70 years later, in 1970, the London *Daily Mirror* sponsored the World Cup Rally over the 16,000 miles between London and Mexico City, where that year's World Cup football championship was to be played. That was the longest rally ever held.

In the intervening years, and since then, automobiles have been grist to the reporter's mill, whether they are covering a race or a rally, the launching of a new car, industrial problems in factories, or merely reporting motoring statistics.

Some of the most fascinating and indicative statistics reported about the motor industry are very revealing about the changing habits and expectations of society. A survey compiled in 1971, for example, showed that there were over 232 million motor vehicles registered in the world, and over 181 million of these were cars. Population per vehicle was 15. The USA was top of the list, having almost half the cars and over a third of the commercial vehicles. There, the distribution was 1.9 people for every vehicle, whereas in the USSR the number was 43.

The biggest producer of motor vehicles has consistently been the USA. In 1935 almost four million vehicles were built while the next biggest producer, the United Kingdom, produced only 416,899, one tenth as many. Fifteen years later the gap had increased still more, the USA producing just over eight million, the United Kingdom a little under 800,000. Twenty years after that, however, things had changed radically. The UK dropped from second to fifth largest producer, the USA increased its output only marginally, and Japan, whose production had been just 31,597 twenty years previously, was now in second place, manufacturing nearly 5,300,000 vehicles.

WORLD LAND SPEED RECORD

Establishing a world record has been the aim of countless drivers – and so has setting out to break it again. Perhaps the greatest challenge is the World Land Speed Record. Its story is also that of the progress of automobile technology, for while any really keen enthusiast could try for the record in the early days, in more recent years a huge financial investment has been necessary, as specially constructed jet-propelled machines have come to replace conventional piston-engined vehicles.

The first of the line of 38 record-holders was Comte Gaston de Chasseloup-Laubat, who in 1898 reached 39.24mph in his electric Jeantaud. For the next year he and Camille Jenatzy, who also drove an electric vehicle, named *La Jamais Contente*, held the record turn and turn about, three times each, pushing it up to 65.79mph. Then the record passed to a steam-driven vehicle, owned by L. Serpollet, who reached 75.06mph in 1902. Only later that year did a petrol-engined car take the coveted prize for the first time, when W. K. Vanderbilt Jr travelled at 76.08mph.

The first person to top 100mph was L. E. Rigolly, who reached 103.56mph in a 100-hp Gobron-Brillié at Ostend, Belgium. After the First World War the challenge became even more specialist; the record was broken for the last time on the special track at Brooklands in May 1922, and on an ordinary road two years later. Malcolm Campbell achieved 150.87mph on Pendine Sands, Wales, in 1925 in a 350-hp V-12 Sunbeam. H. O. D. Segrave reached 200mph two years later at Daytona Beach, Florida, in a twin-engined 1000hp Sunbeam. In

1935, 301.13mph was reached by Campbell in his specially constructed *Bluebird* on Bonneville Salt Flats near Salt Lake City, Utah. All future attempts on the record except one were to take place there.

Not until 1963 was the 400mph barrier breached, when Craig Breedlove achieved 407.45mph in his jet-powered, three-wheeled *Spirit of America*. His claim to the record was disallowed, however. The authorities argued that *Spirit of America* was a motorcycle, not a car. They changed their minds the following year, but not before Donald Campbell (son of Malcolm) had driven at 403.10mph in *Bluebird-Proteus*. In 1964, Craig Breedlove travelled at 526.28mph in *Spirit of America*, and the following year achieved 600.6 mph in *Spirit of America Sonic I*.

The current record-holder is Gary Gabelich who reached 630.38mph in *Blue Flame* in 1970. The record for a piston-engined car is held by *Goldenrod*, driven by Robert Summers at 418.5 mph at Bonneville in November 1965.

THE FIRST RACES

Amid all the media publicity that surrounds the race for the World Championship each year, we should not forget the man who started it all: James Gordon Bennett. Although the rules laid down for his cup were rather restrictive, the races were the first international events. Entries were by national rather than manufacturers' teams, and every part of each car entered had to be built, though not necessarily designed, in the country it represented. Even the exasperating oddities of the rules helped, since they stimulated the organization of the first Grand Prix in 1906.

The first Gordon Bennett race was held in 1900. Five cars entered from France, Belgium and the United States. Only two of these finished. Six years later there were eighteen cars from six nations.

THE MEN AT THE WHEEL

Years of design and engineering experience, substantial financial sponsorship and a devoted back-up team are all essential for success in Grand Prix racing. But in the final analysis victory or defeat hangs on the skills and judgment of the man at the wheel. There can scarcely be a driver who has not added something to the sport. These are just a few of the best-known record breakers.

Jackie Stewart, world champion in 1973, the year he retired, won more victories in world championship racing than any other driver, coming in first 27 times in 99 races.

Juan-Manuel Fangio became world champion in 1951, and again each year from 1954 to 1957. He won 24 Grands Prix out of the 51 he entered, and in the 1957 German Grand Prix broke the lap record no less than ten times.

Stirling Moss was never a world champion, but he ranks as one of the world's greatest drivers, having scored over 100 victories in fourteen years' racing.

Graham Hill, world champion in 1962 and 1968, raced in more Grands Prix than any other driver, 176 in all, winning fourteen of them (including the Monaco Grand Prix five times). In the early 1970s he ran his own team until he was killed in an air crash in 1975.

Tazio Nuvolari started racing in 1920 at the age of 28, and for the first years of his career concentrated on motor-cycles. His great years in motor-racing were the early 1930s, when he mostly drove for Alfa Romeo, winning not only Grands Prix but also sports car races. He retired from racing in the late 1940s.

Bernard Rosemeyer drove for Auto Union for just three seasons (he was killed in early 1938 in a speed record attempt). He won his first Grand Prix at the end of his first season, triumphed in no less than five in 1936 and did very well in 1937 against much tougher opposition from Mercedes.

MODERN TIMES

In performance, styling and safety features, today's cars
take much from the models built for the racetrack.
Shown here is the Aston Martin Lagonda, first marketed
in 1977. In super-speed and luxury it points to the 1980s.

Two successful family cars of the immediate post-war period are shown here. The Volvo PV444 (*top*) was developed after the Swedish company switched its efforts in 1944 to the production of a smaller car. The P444 continued to be manufactured until 1965, although by that time its engine size had increased from 1.4 to 1.8 litres, and a 5-speed instead of the original 3-speed gearbox had been installed. The PV444 started Volvo on the road to success as an internationally known automobile manufacturer and was their first car to be sold widely outside Scandinavia.

Below is a 1948 model from Chrysler, one of the American automobile giants. This 'Town and Country' 5.3-litre sedan came into production in 1946 and had a wooden exterior trim.

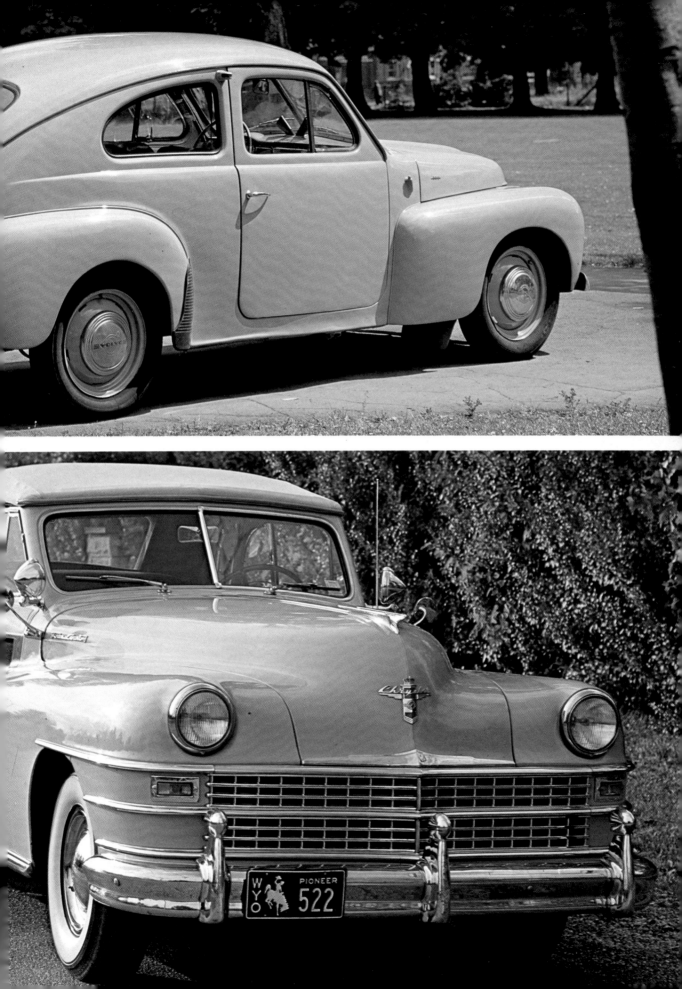

The Mercedes Benz 300 SL (*left*) was in production from 1954 to 1963 and had its genesis in the 1952 SL sports racing car. Its futuristic looks were appealing, and 3250 cars were sold. The 300 SL was made in two versions, first the gull-wing, shown here, and then, from 1957, the open-top roadster. The doors of the gull-wing opened along the top edge.

Below left is a 1954 Ferrari 860 Monza, one of the series of 4-cylinder sports cars developed in the mid-1950s from the company's Formula 2 racing cars. They did not have much competition success.

The 1955 Austin-Healey 100 (*below*) was the production version of the two-seater sports Healey Hundred, which was first displayed at the 1952 London Motor Show. Its production was taken over by Austin shortly afterwards.

Chrysler's distinctive 300 range, which first came on to the market in 1955, was designed to put the company well out in front of its rivals. It was conceived as a particular challenge to Ford's Thunderbird (*see opposite*). The series was manufactured with great success for ten years in many different versions (shown below is the 1960 300K). When it was first produced, the 300 had a three-speed automatic gearbox and push-button controls. Its maximum speed was an aggressive 130mph, which did indeed fulfill the company's hopes for it.

The 4.8-litre Thunderbird two-seater sports car (*above right*), launched in 1954 and available the following year, heralded Ford's return to the sporting scene. It was spurred on by the Chevrolet Corvette, launched two years before. The cars were cleanly styled and all of them had V8 engines. The Thunderbird remained a pure sports cars for three years, during which over 53,000 were built. Thereafter it was transformed into a clumsier four-seater and lost much of its specialist appeal.

The Chevrolet Corvette can justly be called *the*

post-war American two-seater sports car. It came on the market in 1953 and has been on sale ever since. It was challenged only by the Ford Thunderbird in the mid-1950s. Three different styles have succeeded each other. The second was the Stingray, shown here (*bottom*). Nearly 118,000 were built between 1962 and 1967 and were very popular and greatly praised. The Stingray had all-independent suspension. Four-wheel disc brakes were introduced in 1965, and a 7-litre engine became available in 1966.

The 2-litre super-powerful Lotus Elite is one of
the first cars built almost entirely by Lotus
rather than being assembled from different
manufacturers' parts. Shown above is a 1974
model. The 2-litre model replaced the Elan
Plus Two and became the first of a new range,
among them the Eclat and the Esprit. The
Elite has a glassfibre body, a five-speed gearbox
and all-independent suspension modelled on
that of racing cars. Its maximum speed is over
120mph but fuel consumption is low because the
car is so light.

Colin Chapman, Lotus's founder, built his first
car in 1948, formed a company four years later
and has been in business ever since. His
production models reflect his race track
experience.

The Rolls-Royce Silver Shadow was first
marketed in 1965. It underwent substantial
modifications six years later. Some 30,000 of
both versions have been built. A 1974 model is
shown here.

Ten years' development work went into the
Silver Shadow, the first Rolls-Royce to have
four-wheel disc brakes, independent rear
suspension and a sensitive self-levelling system
that even compensates for the gradual emptying
of the fuel tank. Like all its stable-mates, the
Silver Shadow is built with meticulous attention
to detail. The bodyshell receives at least twelve
coats of primer and paint and much of the
interior is hand built. Standard features include
stereo and quadrophonic tape-playing
equipment.

Left: 1978 Porsche 911SC Targa. The 911 went into production in 1964, and since then over 165,000 have been built. The current version, the 911SC has a 3-litre engine and is the most powerful of the series.

The original Ford GTs made their first race appearance in 1964 without much success, although they more than made up for this later. The production cars came on the market in the following year and almost all were sold for use in competitions. Only a handful were actually built for road use. *Below left* is the 1965 GT 40.

Lister cars had MG or Bristol engines at first but changed to Jaguars in 1957. That year the car won four major events. In 1958 a 3-litre version and a single-seater were built. No more were produced after 1959, the year in which the model shown below was built.

The Mini falls into that rare category – a really revolutionary car that started a new trend and found countless imitators around the world. Its designer, Alec Issigonis, had already designed the highly popular Morris Minor, which remained in production for over twenty years. But his aim in this case was to produce a completely new economy car, and he succeeded brilliantly. His design called for a transverse engine, front-wheel drive and all-round independent suspension: it produced magnificent road-holding and handling. Here at last was an economical car far removed from the slow-moving 'old lady' image of previous cheap models, and it came just at the moment when increasing prosperity meant more and more families were buying second cars and young people were anxious to own a car.

First produced as part of the Austin and Morris ranges, Minis are now a British Leyland marque (shown above is a 1978 Clubman Estate). The cars have been manufactured in numerous versions and have had considerable competition success in the form of the Cooper S, taking part in international rallies, touring car races etc.

Above right: 1975 Volkswagen 'Beetle'. With about 20 million sold, this is the most successful car of all time (even outstripping the Ford Model T by some five million), a remarkable fact considering its origins as Nazi Germany's 'people's car'. Production never started before the outbreak of war and many German citizens paid deposits for cars they were never to see, but after the war production increased as rapidly as circumstances would permit. Reliable, strong and unfashionable in its looks, the 'Beetle' remains immensely popular, although very few are now being manufactured.

Below right: Datsun's 240Z range was announced in 1969 and had immediate sporting and commercial success. In 1971 it took first, second and seventh place in the East African Safari and won two Manufacturer's Championships in the USA. The 260Z was marketed in 1974 and a 2.8-litre version is available in the USA (shown here is the 1972 sports coupé). In the last decade, Japanese cars have sold increasingly well in Europe, chiefly because of their reputation for quality and low price.

Custom-built

Customized cars are a trend of the 1970s, a time when the economics of motor-manufacturing demand increasing standard-ization and the production of reliable, reasonably priced cars in large quantities. Such mass-produced cars may suit the family motorist down to the ground but they leave no room for individual expression and enthusiasm. Customizing a car firmly establishes an eye-catching identity for it, and consequently for its owner. In so doing it marks a conscious attempt to imitate the earliest days of motoring, when owners cherished their vehicles as individual personalities. Three custom designs are shown here:

Top left is a V8 engine installed in a customized replica of a Ford Model T.

Bottom left is an Australian treatment of a 1956 Ford 100E.

The Chevrolet Corvette Stingray (see also page 47) is a fine example of the customizer's imagination and graphic skills (*below*). The first Stingray purchasers were buying a highly personal car. It has been very popular with American automobile enthusiasts for well over 20 years. Now the customizer can maintain that tradition.

RACING

Grand Prix racing has seen enormous changes since the war. Speeds have increased, the cars' weights have decreased, safety is better ensured, the drivers have become media superstars – but the thrill of the track remains the same. The 1950 HWM Jaguar-engined Formula 2 car opposite introduces modern racing. HWM's team included the young Stirling Moss and Peter Collins.

Dragster racing is in one sense the ultimate form of motor sport. Specially built cars, useless for any other purpose, race each other two at a time down a quarter-mile drag strip. Pairs of cars are started about every half minute, and as many as 1000 runs can be seen in one day's competition.

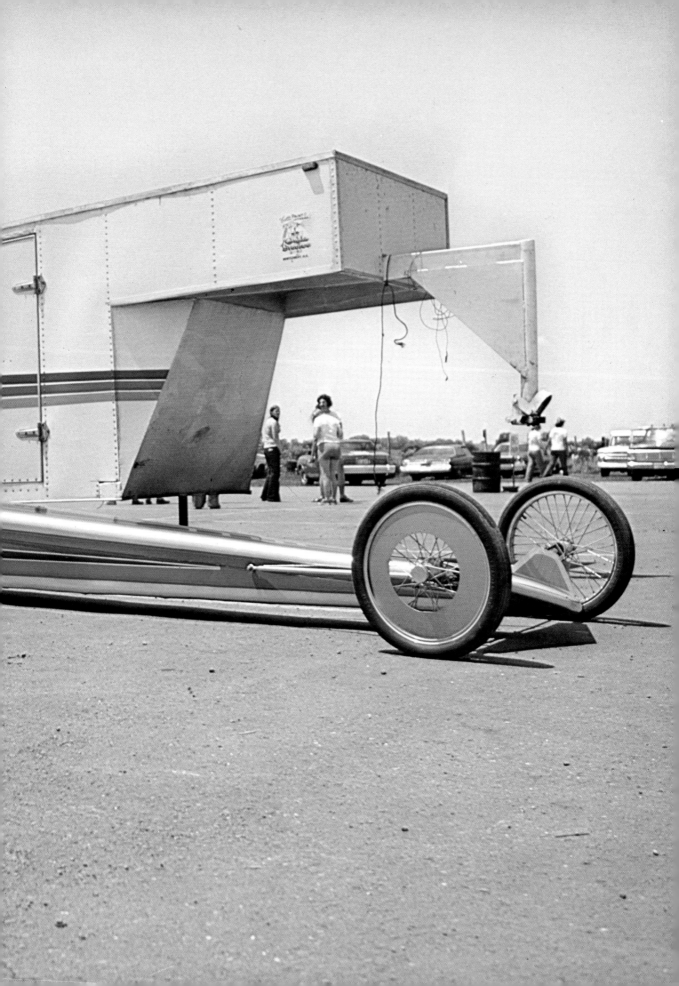

James Hunt (*top left*), the British Grand Prix racing-driver, at the wheel of the Marlboro-McLaren he drove during the 1977 season. Hunt became World Champion in 1976 when he won seven championship races (two were later disallowed, one of which was later still reinstated). He won three championship Grands Prix in 1977 – the British, Japanese and US – and also the Race of Champions. The present Formula 1 regulations have been in force since January 1966 and allow for a maximum engine capacity of 3 litres unsupercharged, 1.5 supercharged.

This Formula Super-Vee racing car (*centre left*) was built for the German Bosch racing team (the Vee stands for Volkswagen). For Super-Vee racing, supercharged VW1600 engines are installed in single-seater chassis; the other components – gearbox, suspension, steering – must be standard.

Below left is a two-seater car used in the European Hill-Climbing Championship. This is a series of about a dozen mountain races, mainly on closed public roads.

Sports car racing often involves a stop in the pits for refuelling. Speed is therefore absolutely essential and here (*below*) highly experienced mechanics work flat out to get the car away again and back into the race.

'Hot rod' cars, like the one shown above, are production models that are so highly modified that no ordinary motorist would feel at home behind the wheel. The bumpers are removed, and so are the glass and the passenger door. Interior roll bars, to strengthen the car should it turn over, are compulsory. 'Hot-rod' racing is a development of stock-car racing. For these events, production car bodies, with only the driver's seat remaining, are attached to a separate chassis with, for Formula 1, a six-cylinder engine.

Opposite : Denny Hulme drives a McLaren M6B in the Canadian-American Challenge Cup (Can-Am), the road-racing championship held on eight circuits in the United States and Canada. Can-Am was started in 1966, and for the first years McLaren cars, driven either by Bruce McLaren himself or by his fellow New Zealander, Denny Hulme, were always dominant. They took the championship every year from 1967 to 1971. Although the championship is still held, professional and public interest has waned. Porsche's entry into the championship enormously raised the cost of competing, and so racing teams began to concentrate on the high-speed events held on special tracks, which are also more popular.

INDEX

First published in 1979 by
Galley Press in association with
Cathay Books
59 Grosvenor Street, London W1

ISBN 0 86178 014 0

© 1979 Cathay Books

Produced by
Mandarin Publishers Limited
22a Westlands Road,
Quarry Bay, Hong Kong

Printed in Singapore.

PDO 79-152